Guess who has the manners.

MANNERS

ALIKI

GREENWILLOW BOOKS, NEW YORK

j 395
(1)

Watercolor paints, colored pencils, and a black pen were used for the full-color art. The text type is ITC
Symbol; hand lettering was done by the artist. Copyright © 1990 by Aliki Brandenberg. All rights reserved.
No part of this book may be reproduced or utilized in any form or by any means, electronic or mechanical,
including photocopying, recording, or by any information storage and retrieval system, without permis-
sion in writing from the Publisher, Greenwillow Books, a division of William Morrow & Company, Inc.,
105 Madison Avenue, New York, NY 10016. Printed in Hong Kong by South China Printing Company
(1988) Ltd. First Edition   1 2 3 4 5 6 7 8 9 10

Library of Congress Cataloging-in-Publication Data
Aliki.   Manners / Aliki.   p.   cm.
Summary: Discusses manners and gives examples of good manners and bad manners.
ISBN 0-688-09198-9. ISBN 0-688-09199-7 (lib. bdg.)
1. Etiquette for children and teenagers.   [1. Etiquette.]   I. Title.
BJ1857.C5A39 1990   395′.122–dc20   89-34622   CIP   AC

For my mother,
Stella Lagakos Liacouras

MANNERS

WHAT ARE MANNERS?

Manners are the way people behave.

Manners are the way you treat others.

Good manners  make you nice.

They make others want to be with you.

With good manners, you are polite.

You are thoughtful and considerate.

Manners are WORDS and ACTIONS that show others you CARE

WHAT BABIES DON'T KNOW

Babies are not born with manners.

They do not know how to say *Please!*

or *Thank you!* or *I'd like my Teddy!* or *I'm sleepy!*

Babies cry for things because they can't talk.

But babies grow into children, and learn.

They learn manners so others will want them around.

NOBODY LIKES TANTRUMS!

GREETINGS

How do you do?

Good Morning, Mrs. Lambros.

Hello!

Please come in.

Please have a seat.

Would you like a drink?

It was a pleasure to meet you. Goodbye.

It was nice to see you again. Goodbye.

Goodbye. See you tomorrow!

Have a good day!

ha ha

WHAT ELENA KNOWS

Please may I lick the bowl? I promise to eat all my supper!

"Please" goes a long way.

For that, Elena will probably get a cookie, too.

MANNERS LESSON #1

Aunt Bessie Doesn't Have to Know Everything

YOU ARE INTERRUPTING AGAIN, LEON

I'M SORRY

MANNERS LESSON #2

The Sand Castle

THE GRABBER

MANNERS LESSON #3
Too Loud Is Too Loud

LOOK AT DANIEL

DON'T YOU WISH YOU DIDN'T HAVE TO?

Here's a hanky, Daniel.

HOW ANTHONY ALMOST RUINED DIANA'S PARTY

Anthony never says hello.

He has no manners.

He embarrasses.

He makes fun.

He's a bad sport.

He cheats.

He bites.

He calls people names.

He grabs.

He tattles.

He throws food.

He's rude.

He didn't even say good-bye.

Nobody missed him.

He almost ruined my party.

But he didn't.

GOSSIP
and
WHISPERS

NOBODY'S PERFECT

OUCH

Here comes Alexa.
Let's ignore her.

Bad manners
and
bad feelings.

Is Alexa
going to go
home and cry?

MANNERS LESSON #4

At the Table

seen but not heard.

MANNERS LESSON #5

Part One: Wrong Number

Part Two: Telephone Talk

MANNERS LESSON #6

Traveling

PLEASE, I CAN HELP

A lack of manners
in certain places
can bother others
and cause red faces.

PARDON AND EXCUSE ME

MANNERS LESSON #7

Sleep-over

EVERYBODY MISSES YOU

That's nice to know.

AND NOW FOR SOME ETIQUETTE

AFTER YOU

Wait for the hostess to begin before you do.

Offer others before you help yourself.

Wait for everyone to finish before you clear the table.

Let others enter before you.

Speak only after someone has finished.

Wait for your turn. It will come.

AFTER YOU means you think of others before you think of yourself.

THANK YOU AGAIN

A letter is like a book.
It can be read again and again and again....

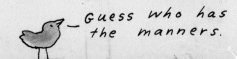